HIPPOPOTAMUS

Jen Green

Grolier
an imprint of

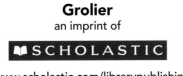

www.scholastic.com/librarypublishing

Published 2009 by Grolier
An imprint of Scholastic Library Publishing
Old Sherman Turnpike, Danbury,
Connecticut 06816

For The Brown Reference Group plc
Project Editor: Jolyon Goddard
Picture Researcher: Clare Newman
Designers: Dave Allen, Jeni Child, John
Dinsdale, Lynne Ross, Sarah Williams
Managing Editors: Bridget Giles, Tim Harris

Volume ISBN-13: 978-0-7172-6297-7
Volume ISBN-10: 0-7172-6297-9

**Library of Congress
Cataloging-in-Publication Data**

Nature's children. Set 4.
    p. cm.
  Includes bibliographical references and
index.
  ISBN 13: 978-0-7172-8083-4
  ISBN 10: 0-7172-8083-7 ((set 4) : alk. paper)
  1. Animals--Encyclopedias, Juvenile. I.
Grolier (Firm)
  QL49.N385 2009
  590.3--dc22
                            2007046315

Printed and bound in China

PICTURE CREDITS

Front Cover: **Nature PL**: Tony Heald.

Back Cover: **Nature PL**: Tony Heald;
Shutterstock: Kaspar Grinvalds, Johan
Swanepoel, Jan Zoetekouw.

FLPA: Gerard Lacz 6; **Nature PL**: Karl
Ammann 2–3, 45, Richard Du Toit 33, Brent
Hedges 18, Andrew Parkinson 22, Peter
Scoones 17, Anup Shah 38, 41, 46;
Photolibrary.com: Hilary Pooley 13;
Shutterstock: Gerrit De Vries 37, EcoPrint
5, 26–27, Vladimir Kondrachov 9, Welland Lau
4, Joaquin Ayllon Perez 30, Vova Pomortzeff
14, Johan Swanepoel 34, Gary Unwin 21;
Still Pictures: Michel and Christine Denis-
Huot/BIOS 10, S. Meyers 42, F. Poelking 29.

Contents

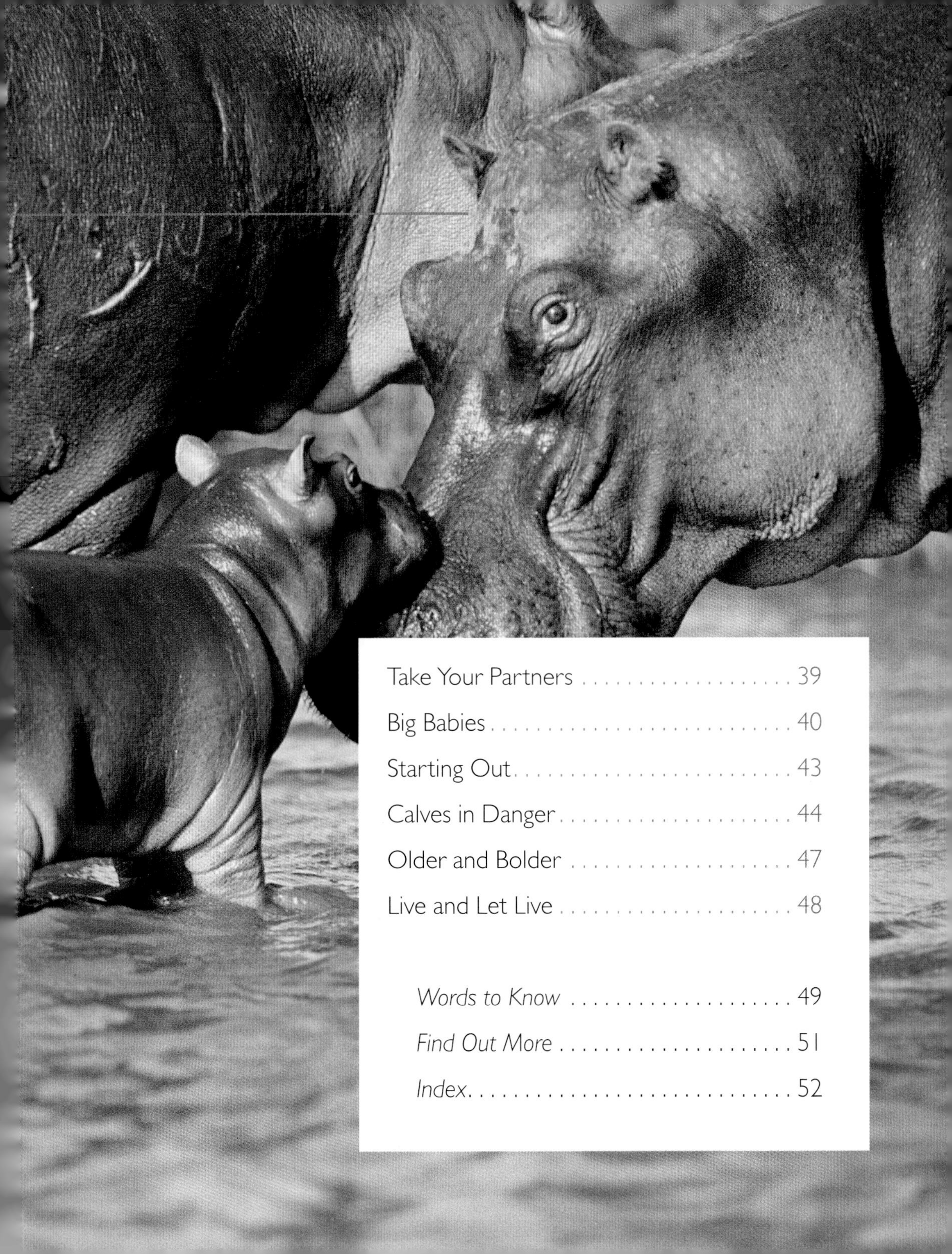

FACT FILE: Hippopotamus

Class	Mammals (Mammalia)
Order	Even-toed hoofed animals (Artiodactyla)
Family	Hippopotamus family (Hippopotamidae)
Genera	*Hippopotamus* and *Hexaprotodon*
Species	Common hippopotamus (*Hippopotamus amphibius*) and pygmy hippopotamus (*Hexaprotodon liberiensis*)
World Distribution	Africa
Habitat	Grasslands near water; pygmy hippos live in forests
Distinctive physical characteristics	Barrel-shaped body; large head with small eyes and ears; short legs and tail; common hippos have grayish-brown skin with a pinkish underside; pygmy hippos have dark gray skin and a creamy gray underside
Habits	Common hippos are sociable and spend a lot of time in water; pygmy hippos live alone or in twos or threes; hippos feed mostly at night
Diet	Vegetation

Introduction

Which large, lumbering land beast becomes graceful when it takes to the water? The answer is a hippopotamus! Hippos are among the largest of all land animals. With their massive body and big head, they look clumsy on land. However, in the water, where hippos spend most of their time, they are swift and smooth.

Most hippos spend their life in herds, grazing on plants. Female hippos are usually gentle creatures. The males, however, can be very fierce, fighting with their huge tusklike teeth.

The ancient Egyptians worshiped a goddess called Taweret, who was part hippo and part human.

A pygmy hippo grazes.
Pygmy and common hippos
shared a common ancestor
about 8 million years ago.

Hippo Relatives

The word *hippopotamus* means "river horse" in Greek. Hippos are only distantly related to horses. Both hippos and horses belong to the large family of hoofed **mammals**. Within this group, horses belong to the odd-toed hoofed mammals. Horses have just one toe on each foot. Hippos, however, have four toes on each foot and, therefore, are even-toed hoofed mammals. This group also includes pigs, cattle, deer, and camels. Many experts believe that pigs are the closest even-toed relatives of hippos. However, some scientists now think that hippos have an even closer relative—whales! They think hippos and whales shared a common land-living ancestor about 54 million years ago.

The hippo family has just two types, or **species**. They are the common, or river, hippo and its smaller relative, the pygmy hippo.

Hippo Country

Hippopotamuses are found only in Africa. **Fossils** from about one million years ago show that there were several more species of hippos, living in Europe and Asia. However, these species became extinct, or died out, leaving just the African hippos.

The common hippo is the more widespread species. It lives in many parts of western, central, and southern Africa. The pygmy hippo is only found on the western tip of Africa. The two species also live in somewhat different places, or habitats. Common hippos inhabit grasslands— anywhere near water, including rivers, lakes, and marshes. Pygmy hippos live in dense, swampy forests.

A herd of common hippos keeps cool in a river.

Common hippos usually live up
to about 30 years in the wild.
In captivity, they sometimes
reach 55 to 60 years.

Heavyweights

The common hippo is among the heaviest land mammals. Only African and Asian elephants and the occasional white rhino are heavier. A big male, or **bull**, hippo stands 5 feet (1.5 m) tall and measures 15 feet (4.5 m) long. He can weigh more than 3 tons (3 tonnes). A female hippo, or **cow**, is smaller and weighs quite a bit less. Being large and heavy has one big advantage: there are few other animals adult hippos need to fear.

Pygmy hippos are only about a third of the size of common hippos. They stand less than 3 feet (1 m) tall and measure 5 feet (1.5 m) long. At about 600 pounds (275 kg) they weigh only a fraction of their larger relatives.

Big but Not Slow

Hippos are unmistakable. With their huge square muzzle, big head, and large barrel-shaped body, it is difficult to confuse a hippo with any other animal. Their eyes and ears are small. Their legs are short but sturdy. The hippo's four toes are protected by black "toenails," which are actually miniature hooves. The hippo's rounded backside ends in a small, tufty tail.

Common hippos are grayish-brown. Their skin is pink on the underside and among the folds in the skin. Pygmy hippos are a darker gray with a creamy underside.

As it lumbers along the riverbank, a hippo's belly almost touches the ground. Still, a hippo can move pretty fast on land. If it needs to, the hippo breaks into a gallop, reaching 25 miles (40 km) per hour. That's pretty impressive for such a heavy and clumsy-looking beast!

Hippos might wander up
to 2 miles (3 km) away
from water to find fresh
food at night.

Bulging eyes on the
sides of the head allow
a hippo to see almost
all around itself.

At Home in Water

Although hippos spend plenty of time on land, they are much more at home in water. Slow-moving rivers and lakes are a hippo's favorite hangouts. They spend much of their time in water partly to keep cool and partly because they feel safe there. If danger threatens, a hippo on land heads straight for the river, while a swimming hippo heads out into deeper water.

A hippo's whole body is built for swimming. It swims in a dog-paddle style. Its feet are webbed. That means the toes are joined with skin, which provides a larger paddling surface. The water supports the animal's great weight, making the hippo more agile.

The hippo's ears, eyes, and nostrils are all located on the top of its head. That way, it can breathe, see, and hear while most of its body is hidden underwater. With just the top of its head showing, most other land animals do not notice the hippo.

Underwater Walk

Hippos are not only expert swimmers, they are also excellent divers. Their large lungs hold enough oxygen to allow them to spend up to six minutes underwater before having to come up for air.

When crossing a river, a hippo usually walks along the bottom on its toes. It uses the air in its lungs to adjust its **buoyancy**, or ability to float. With its lungs full of air, the animal bobs at the surface. With less air in its lungs, it sinks deeper, so it can move along the bottom. As the hippo dives, its nostrils close. The ears fold over to keep water out, too. When the hippo scrambles out of the water onto land, it wiggles its ears energetically to shake off any water on them.

Hippos have very dense, heavy bones. The weight of the bones helps the animal sink when it walks along the riverbed.

A coating of mud protects
a hippo from sunburn as
it feeds on land.

Sensitive Skin

Hippopotamuses have thick, tough skin. However, the outer layer of skin is thin and sensitive. The hippo can, therefore, easily dry out or get sunburned.

Hippos protect their skin by spending a lot of time in water. That keeps the hippo's skin moist and shields it from the harsh sunlight. A reddish-brown liquid seeps from the skin if the animal is out of water for too long. In the past, people used to think that hippos sweated blood. In fact, the reddish liquid is not blood, but a natural oil that keeps the skin moist and supple. It also helps the hippo to heal if it gets scratched or wounded.

All mammals have some hair on their body, and hippos are no exception. At first sight they look almost hairless. However, upon close inspection there is a scattering of fine hairs all over the body. Long, bristly hairs grow on the muzzle and also on the stumpy tail.

Mouthful of Teeth

A hippopotamus has 38 to 42 teeth in its giant mouth. That's more than adult humans—they have just 32 teeth.

A hippo can open its mouth wider than any other mammal, to show off its different kinds of teeth. Broad, ridged back teeth called **molars** are used to grind food to a pulp. The largest teeth are the long, curving **canines**, which grow up from the lower jaw. These tusklike teeth are strong enough to crush a crocodile! Male hippos have longer tusks than females. They use them to battle with other males.

Like a beaver's front teeth, the hippo's canines never stop growing. One hippo canine measured 25 inches (64 cm)! Like elephant tusks, hippo tusks are made of ivory. Illegal hunters, or poachers, sometimes kill hippos to sell their ivory tusks, which are carved into ornaments.

A hippo can open its mouth as wide as 150 degrees!

African people used to make shields and whips from hippos' skin.

Hungry Hippos

Hippos are **herbivores**, or plant eaters. Pygmy hippos eat roots, fruit, grass, and shoots. A common hippo's favorite food is marsh grass.

The hippo's stomach contains several chambers to help digest, or break down, its tough food. Hippos eat a lot of plants. An adult will munch through 88 pounds (40 kg) of food each evening. That may sound like a lot, but in fact, it's not an enormous amount for such a huge beast. The hippo has a slow, lazy lifestyle. The upside of being lazy is that the hippo doesn't need to eat as much food as it would if it were always on the move.

Keeping Alert

Hippos spend much of their day snoozing. The animal might not look alert, but a napping hippo is still aware of its surroundings.

Hippos have sharp hearing. Their small ears can pick up even faint noises. Sounds travel a long way both below and directly above the water's surface. That allows a hippo to be aware of what is happening on the opposite side of a wide river or lake.

Scientists are divided on how well hippos can see. Some experts believe they see well, while other evidence suggests they only see things clearly up close. There's no doubt hippos have a sharp sense of smell. However, they cannot use this sense underwater.

A Hippo's Day

Hippopotamuses aren't very active by day. Common hippos spend much of their day in water, dozing or swimming about lazily. Pygmy hippos spend less time in water, but they do like to lounge around in shallow, muddy pools called **wallows**.

Hippos feed mostly at night. At dusk, they leave the water and make their way to their favorite feeding grounds. They travel along familiar trails that have been worn by generations of hippopotamuses. They usually only go a mile or so from the lake or river. Sometimes, however, they have to go much farther to reach food. At such times, the hippos will stop off at wallows to refresh themselves. They stay at the feeding grounds for about five hours and then head back to the river or lake for a long, relaxing nap.

Animals—such as hippos—that
can live both on land and in water
are called amphibious.

Helping Hippos

Hippos get along well with many other types of animals. They form a kind of partnership with a delicate bird called a cattle egret. These long-legged birds perch on a hippo's back and pick off ticks and flies. Both animals benefit from this arrangement. The egret gets a free meal, and the hippo is rid of pests that infest its skin and suck its blood.

The hippo also has other helpers. Certain kinds of fish swim alongside and feed on **algae**—tiny plantlike living things—that grow on the hippo's skin. That helps keep the hippo's skin healthy. In turn, the hippo helps other animals. Young crocodiles and terrapins sometimes climb onto a hippo's broad back to rest and sunbathe.

The cattle egret picks pests off hippos, zebras, elephants, buffalo, and—as its name suggests—cattle.

A large herd of
hippos gathers
in a river in the
Masai Mara
reserve in Kenya.

Solitary or Sociable?

Common hippos like company. Most females and their young live in herds of 10 to 20 animals. The biggest herds contain as many as 100 hippos. The group is led by several experienced cows. Bulls live outside the herd, although they might be allowed into the herd during the **breeding season**.

The hippos in a herd "talk" to one another using different noises. An excited hippo neighs like a horse. An angry hippo roars, squeals, and bellows. A female hippo who is ready to **mate** moos like a cow!

Pygmy hippos are less sociable. They live alone or in groups of two or three. These mammals are very shy. They run off into the forest at the first sign of danger. Scientists know very little about these wary, woodland mammals.

Enter at Your Peril

Each bull hippo has his own **territory**—a stretch of riverbank that he calls home. A hippo's territory is also called a **refuge**. The biggest, strongest bulls hold the refuges that are next to the herd of cows and their young.

Cows are allowed to enter a bull's refuge, but other males are strictly forbidden. The bull marks the borders of his territory with dung, which he scatters by wagging his tail furiously. These smelly piles send a clear signal to other bulls: "Trespassers are not welcome!" The bull joins the cows briefly for mating, but only with their permission. Even then, if he doesn't behave properly, the cows will attack and drive him away.

A fearsome bull charges toward an intruder in the water.

In Africa, more humans are killed by hippos than by lions. That's mainly because people tend to live near lakes and rivers, where hippos live, too.

Gentle Giants?

Despite their huge bulk, hippopotamuses are generally peaceful animals. Cows and their young get along together well. Young hippos might get out of line occasionally, but their mothers are quick to get them back in line. The cows are usually docile, but mothers are fiercely protective of their babies. Humans have been attacked when they have accidentally come between a cow and her young.

Male hippos are another story. They can be fierce and aggressive particularly in the breeding season. The prime refuges nearest the herd are occupied by the strongest bulls. If a young male wants the chance to mate, he must win control of one of these refuges—and the only way to do that is through a fierce fight!

The Big Fight

A yawning hippo can open its mouth amazingly wide. Like humans, hippos yawn when they are tired. A bull also yawns to show off his teeth to another male when he wants to frighten him away. He will also rear up and make a short charge at his rival, while roaring, bellowing, and snorting water through his nostrils. It's a scary sight, and most intruders back away!

If the rival doesn't take the hint and retreat, a fight breaks out. The pair charge at each other with gaping mouths. Water flies everywhere as each animal slashes at his enemy's head and neck with his long canine tusks. Severe wounds are sometimes inflicted during these fights, and many bulls have the scars to prove it. These battles can last for more than an hour.

A powerful bull hippo with the refuge nearest the cows might keep his territory for up to eight years.

A bull and cow get to know each other. Hippos often make an excited "wheeze-honking" noise during courtship.

Take Your Partners

At about six years old, a female hippopotamus is ready to mate for the first time. At about the same age, bulls are ready, too. However, a young bull needs to win a refuge close to the herd to get the chance to breed. Even then, a male who has beaten a rival does not automatically get to mate. The cow makes the final decision in choosing a mate. Mating usually takes place in the water.

Hippos can breed at any time of year, but most matings are timed so the young will be born in the rainy season. When rain falls, new grass grows. That means there will be plenty of grass for **grazing** cows. They will be hungry while producing nutritious milk for their young.

Big Babies

About eight months after mating, a cow gets ready to give birth. She leaves the herd and carefully selects a safe place that will make a good nursery. Just one baby, called a **calf**, is born. Some calves are born in the water—especially if there is danger on land—but usually the baby is born on the riverbank.

A newborn common hippo is about 3 feet (1 m) long and weighs as much as 120 pounds (55 kg). Pygmy hippo calves are much smaller.

Calves that are born underwater quickly struggle to the surface to take their first gulp of air. A young calf can only hold its breath for about half a minute. It learns to hold its breath for longer as it gets bigger.

A calf sticks close to its mother for the first two years of its life.

Calves usually nurse, or drink their mother's milk, underwater.

Starting Out

Human babies take many months to learn to sit up, crawl, stand, and finally walk. Hippo calves are different. They can walk, run, and swim just minutes after birth. Calves that are born in the water learn to swim before they can walk.

The mother and her calf spend a couple of weeks on their own. After that, they rejoin the herd. The other experienced cows help keep an eye on the calf when the mother goes off to graze.

Mother and baby spend a lot of time floating and swimming in the river. If the calf gets tired, it scrambles up onto its mother's back for a ride. That is also the safest place to keep out of the way of hungry crocodiles.

Calves in Danger

Adult hippopotamuses have few natural enemies. Their giant bulk protects them from even the fiercest **predators**. Calves, however, have many enemies, including lions, crocodiles, and hyenas. A calf's best defense is to stick close to its mother, who will fight to protect her young.

If a calf strays too far from its mother, she will discipline the youngster with a swat from her big muzzle or even by rolling the young hippo over. If the calf is well behaved, she rewards it with a nuzzle or an affectionate lick.

A calf gets a nuzzle from its mother at Virunga National Park, in the Democratic Republic of the Congo.

Like most baby mammals,
young hippos love to play
with one another.

Older and Bolder

As the calf gets bigger, it starts to play with other young hippos. The babies splash and tumble in the shallows. They squeal and play-fight. They pretend to bite one another and scramble onto one another's backs.

For the first four or five months of life, the calf drinks its mother's milk. After that, it begins to eat grass. At this time it starts to make longer journeys with its mother as she travels inland to find fresh plants to eat.

At about eight years of age, young bulls must leave the herd and set up their own refuge. All the best places near the herd are taken, so the young animals have to move some distance away. When the bulls are older and stronger, they will fight for a better position. Young cows are allowed to stay with the herd.

Live and Let Live

A few centuries ago, hippopotamuses lived in most parts of Africa, wherever there was water. However, in the past few hundred years, people have killed many hippos for their meat, ivory tusks, or just for "sport." There are still many common hippos in the wild, but pygmy hippos have become rare.

Now hippos face a new threat. People are taking over the grasslands, rivers, and forests where hippos live to make new farms, towns, and villages. That results in less habitat suitable for hippos. Luckily, people have also set up parks and reserves where hippos can live, breed, and raise their young in peace. Today, most hippos are found in these protected areas, where they can live long, contented lives.

Words to Know

Algae Tiny plantlike living things that grow in water or moist places.

Breeding season The time of year when animals of the same kind come together to produce young.

Bull A male hippopotamus.

Buoyancy The ability to float in water.

Calf A young hippopotamus.

Canines The long front teeth, or tusks, that hippos use for fighting.

Cow A female hippopotamus.

Fossils The preserved remains of animals and plants that lived millions of years ago.

Grazing Eating grass.

Herbivores	Animals that eat plants.
Mammals	Animals that have hair on their body and nourish their young on milk.
Mate	To come together to produce young; either of a breeding pair of animals.
Molars	The broad back teeth that are used for chewing and grinding food.
Predators	Animals that hunt other animals.
Refuge	The territory of a male hippo.
Species	The scientific word for animals of the same kind that can breed together.
Territory	An area where an animal lives and feeds and which it defends against others of its kind.
Wallows	Shallow pools where hippos rest.

Find Out More

Books

Ring, S. *Project Hippopotamus*. Zoo Life. Calgary, Aberta, Canada: Weigl Educational Publishers Limited, 2003.

Storad, C. J. *Hippos*. Early Bird Nature Books. Minneapolis, Minnesota: Lerner Publishing Group, 2005.

Web sites

Creature Feature: Hippopotamuses
kids.nationalgeographic.com/Animals/CreatureFeature/ Hippopotamus
Pictures and facts about hippos.

Hippopotamus
www.enchantedlearning.com/subjects/mammals/hippo/ Hippoprintout.shtml
Printout of a common hippo to color in.

Index